REINCARNATION

REINCARNATION

ANNIE BESANT

GYAN

Published by

GYAN

Gyan Publishing House
5, Ansari Road
Daryaganj, New Delhi-110002
Phone: 011-47034999, 9811692060
E-mail: books@gyanbooks.com

Distribution Network
gyanbooks.com
India, USA, Canada, UK, Australia

ISBN: 978-93-6780-264-9 (PB)

First Published, 1898

2nd Impression 2024

Printed at: Gyan Press, Delhi.

REINCARNATION
Author: ANNIE BESANT

REINCARNATION

ANNIE BESANT

THEOSOPHICAL PUBLISHING SOCIETY
26 CHARING CROSS S.W.
NEW YORK
65 FIFTH AVENUE
BENARES
THEOSOPHICAL PUBLISHING SOCIETY
1898

Few words are needed in sending this little book out into the world. It is the second of a series of Manuals designed to meet the public demand for a simple exposition of Theosophical teachings. Some have complained that our literature is at once too abstruse, too technical, and too expensive for the ordinary reader, and it is our hope that the present series may succeed in supplying what is a very real want. Theosophy is not only for the learned; it is for all. Perhaps among those who in these little books catch their first glimpse of its teachings, there may be a few who will be led by them to penetrate more deeply into its philosophy, its science, and its religion, facing its abstruser problems with the student's zeal and the neophyte's ardour. But these Manuals are not written for the eager student, whom no initial difficulties can daunt; they are written for the busy men and women of the work-a-day world, and seek to make plain some of the great truths that render life easier to bear and death easier to face. Written by servants of the Masters who are the Elder Brothers of our race, they can have no other object than to serve our fellow-men.

REINCARNATION.

Introduction.

If it be difficult for a new truth to gain a hearing amid the strife of tongues that marks our modern civilisation, it is yet more difficult for a truth to make itself heard, which has become new only by force of age. If our eye could sweep over the intellectual history of the race, unrolled before us for centuries of millenniums, then a gap in the dominance of some world-wide idea, stretching over some few hundreds of years among a small number of the nations, would but slightly impress us. But when that gap—a mere partial fissure in an immemorial past—includes the intellectual development of Europe, and is scanned by Europeans, it assumes an importance quite out of proportion to its relative extent in time, its relative weight in argument. Great and valuable as is the contribution brought by Europe to the mental treasure-house of mankind, we Europeans are very apt to over-estimate it, and to forget that the very brief period of intellectual achievement in Europe cannot rationally be taken as outweighing the total mental fruitage of the non-European races, gathered over thousands of centuries. This looming large of our own recent past, until, as a plate held before our eyes shuts out the sun, it hides the past of the world from our mental gaze, is a danger against which we should be on our guard. Neither for individuals nor for nations is intellectual arrogance synonymous with intellectual stature; the feeling which makes the Englishman look on all dark-skinned races as inferior, and lump them comprehensively as "niggers," from whom nothing can be learned, is a feeling essentially petty and parochial. The wise listen most readily to those whose habits of thought are most alien from their own, knowing that thus they may chance to catch a glimpse of some new aspect of Truth, instead of seeing once more the mere reflection of the aspect already familiar. Men's racial habits, traditions, surroundings, are as coloured glasses through which they look at the sun of Truth; each glass lends its own tint to the sunbeam, and the white ray is transmitted as red, or blue, or yellow—what you will. As we cannot get rid of our glass and catch the pure uncoloured radiance, we do wisely to combine the coloured rays and so obtain the white.

Now Reincarnation is a truth that has swayed the minds of innumerable millions of our race, and has moulded the thoughts of the vast majority for uncounted centuries. It dropped out of the European mind during the Dark Ages, and so ceased to influence our mental and moral development—very much, be it said in passing, to the injury of that development. For the last hundred years it has from time to time flashed through the minds of some of the greater Westerns, as a possible explanation of some of life's most puzzling problems: and during the last dozen years, since its clear enunciation as an essential part of the Esoteric Teaching, it has been constantly debated, and is as constantly gaining ground, among the more thoughtful students of the mysteries of life and of evolution.

There is, of course, no doubt that the great historical religions of the East included the teaching of Reincarnation as a fundamental tenet. In India, as in Egypt, Reincarnation was at the root of ethics. Among the Jews it was held commonly by the Pharisees,[1] and the popular belief comes out in various phrases in the *New Testament*, as when John the Baptist is regarded as a reincarnation of Elijah, or as when the disciples ask whether the man born blind is suffering for the sin of his parents or for some former sin of his own. The *Zohar*, again, speaks of souls as being subjected to transmigration. "All souls are subject to revolution (metempsychosis, *a'leen b'gilgoolah*), but men do not know the ways of the Holy One; blessed be it! they are ignorant of the way they have been judged in all time, and before they came into this world and when they have quitted it."[2] The *Kether Malkuth* evidently has the same idea as that conveyed by Josephus, when it says: "If she (the soul) be pure, then shall she obtain favour and rejoice in the latter day; but if she hath been defiled, then shall she wander for a time in pain and despair".[3] So also, we find the doctrine taught by eminent Fathers of the Church, and Ruffinus[4] states that belief in it was common among the primitive Fathers. Needless to say that the philosophic Gnostics and Neo-Platonists held it as an integral part of their doctrine. If we glance to the Western Hemisphere we meet Reincarnation as a firmly rooted belief among many of the tribes of North and South America. The Mayas,

[1] Josephus, *Antiq.*, xviii. i., § 3, says the virtuous "shall have power to revive and live again".

[2] *Zohar*, ii., fol. 99, *b. sq.* Quoted in Myer's *Qabbalah*, p. 198.

[3] Quoted in Myer's *Qabbalah*, p. 198.

[4] Letter to Anastasius, quoted by E. D. Walker, in *Reincarnation: a Study of Forgotten Truth.*

with their deeply interesting connection in language and symbolism with ancient Egypt, to this day hold the traditional doctrine, as has been shown by the investigations of Dr. and Mme. le Plongeon. To these, the name of many another tribe might be added, remnants of once famous nations, that in their decay have preserved the ancestral beliefs that once linked them with the mightiest peoples of the elder world.

It could scarcely be expected that a teaching of such vast antiquity and such magnificent intellectual ancestry should fade out of the mind of mankind; and accordingly we find that the eclipse it suffered a few centuries ago was very partial, affecting only a small portion of the race. The ignorance that swamped Europe carried away belief in Reincarnation, as it carried away all philosophy, all metaphysics, and all science. Mediæval Europe did not offer the soil on which could flourish any wide-sweeping and philosophical view of man's nature and destiny. But in the East, which enjoyed a refined and gracious civilisation while Europe was sunk in barbarism; which had its philosophers and its poets while the West was densely illiterate; in the East, the great doctrine held undisputed sway, whether in the subtle metaphysics of the Brâhmans, or in the noble morality which finds its home under the shadow of the Buddha and His Good Law.

But while a fact of Nature may in some part of the world for a time be ignored, it cannot be destroyed, and, submerged for a moment, it will again reassert itself in the sight of men. This has been anew demonstrated in the history of the doctrine of Reincarnation in Europe, in its occasional reappearances, traceable from the founding of Christendom to the present time, in its growing acceptance to-day.

When Christianity first swept over Europe, the inner thought of its leaders was deeply tinctured with this truth. The Church tried ineffectually to eradicate it, and in various sects it kept sprouting forth beyond the time of Erigena and Bonaventura, its mediæval advocates. Every great intuitional soul, as Paracelsus, Boehme and Swedenborg, has adhered to it. The Italian luminaries, Giordano Bruno and Campanella, embraced it. The best of German philosophy is enriched by it. In Schopenhauer, Lessing, Hegel, Leibnitz, Herder, and Fichte the younger, it is earnestly advocated. The anthropological systems of Kant and Schelling furnish points of contact with it. The younger Helmont, in *De Revolutione Animarum*, adduces in two hundred problems all the arguments which may be urged in favour of the return of souls into human bodies, according to Jewish ideas. Of English thinkers, the Cambridge Platonists defended it with much learning and acuteness, most conspicuously Henry More; and in Cudworth and Hume it ranks as the most rational theory of immortality. Glanvil's *Lux Orientalis* devotes a curious treatise to it. It captivated the minds of Fourier and Leroux. André Pezzani's book on *The Plurality of the Soul's Lives* works out the system on the Roman Catholic idea of expiation.[1]

The reader of Schopenhauer will be familiar with the aspect taken by Reincarnation in his philosophy. Penetrated as was the great German with Eastern thought from his study of the Upanishads, it would have been passing strange had this corner-stone of Hindu philosophy found no place in his system. Nor is Schopenhauer the only philosopher from the intellectual and mystical German people who has accepted Reincarnation as a necessary factor in Nature. The opinions of Fichte, of Herder, of Lessing, may surely claim to be of some weight in the intellectual world, and these men see in Reincarnation a solution for problems otherwise insoluble. It is true that the intellectual world is not a despotic State, and none may impose his opinion on his fellows by personal authority; none the less are opinions weighed

[1] E. D. Walker, *op. cit.*, pp. 65, 66.

there rather than counted, and the mightier and more instructed intellects of the West, though they be here in a small minority, will command respectful hearing for that which they deliberately advance, from all whose minds are not so hide-bound by modern tradition as to be unable to appreciate the value of arguments addressed to the support of an unfashionable truth.

It is interesting to note that the mere idea of Reincarnation is no longer regarded in the West—at least by educated people—as absurd. It is gradually assuming the position of a possible hypothesis, to be considered on its merits, on its power of explaining puzzling and apparently unrelated phenomena. Regarding it myself as, to me, a proven fact, I am concerned rather to put it forward in these pages as a probable hypothesis, throwing more light than does any other theory on the obscure problems of man's constitution, of his character, his evolution, and his destiny. Reincarnation and Karma are said by a Master to be the two doctrines of which the West stands most in need; so it cannot be ill done for a believer in the Masters to set forth an outline, for the ordinary reader, of this central teaching of the Esoteric Philosophy.

THE MEANING OF REINCARNATION.

Let us start with a clear understanding of what is meant by Reincarnation. So far as the derivation of the word is concerned, any repeated entering into a physical, or fleshly, covering, might be included thereunder. It certainly implies the existence of something relatively permanent that enters into, inhabits, successive somethings relatively impermanent. But the word tells us nothing of the nature of these relatively permanent and impermanent somethings, save that the impermanent habitations are of "flesh". Another word, often used as synonymous with Reincarnation, the word Metempsychosis, suggests the other side of the transaction; here the habitation is ignored, and the stress is laid on the transit of the Psyche, the relatively permanent. Putting the two together as descriptive of the whole idea, we should have the entry of a Psyche or "soul" into successive "bodies" of flesh; and though the word "soul" is open to serious objections, from its looseness and its theological connotations, it may stand for the moment as representing in the minds of most people a form of existence which outlasts the physical frame with which it was connected during a life on earth.

In this general sense, apart from any special exoteric or esoteric teachings, Reincarnation and Metempsychosis are words which denote a theory of existence, according to which a form of visible matter is inhabited by a more ethereal principle, which outlives its physical encasement, and, on the death of the latter, passes on immediately or after an interval, to dwell in some other frame. Never, perhaps, has this doctrine, in its loftiest form, been put more clearly or more beautifully than in the famous encouragement of Arjuna by Krishna, given in the *Bhagavad Gîtâ*:—

> These bodies of the embodied One, who is eternal, indestructible and boundless, are known as finite. . . . He who regardeth this as a slayer, and he who thinketh he is slain, both of them are ignorant. He slayeth not nor is he slain. He is not born, nor doth he die; nor having been, ceaseth he any more to be; unborn, perpetual, eternal and ancient, he is not slain when the body is slaughtered. Who knoweth him indestructible, unborn, undiminishing, how can that man slay, O Pârtha, or cause to be slain? As a man, casting off worn-out garments, taketh new

ones, so the dweller in the body, casting off worn-out bodies, entereth into others that are new. Weapons cleave him not, nor fire burneth him, nor waters wet him, nor wind drieth him away. Indivisible he, incombustible he, and indeed neither to be wetted nor dried away; perpetual, all-pervasive, stable, immovable, ancient, unmanifest, unthinkable, immutable, he is called; therefore knowing him as such thou shouldst not grieve.[1]

The theory of Reincarnation, then, in the Esoteric Philosophy, asserts the existence of a living and individualised Principle, which dwells in and informs the body of a man, and which, on the death of the body, passes into another body, after a longer or shorter interval. Thus successive bodily lives are linked together like pearls strung upon a thread, the thread being the living Principle, the pearls upon it the separate human lives.

What it is that Reincarnates.

Having grasped the idea that Reincarnation is the indwelling of a living something in a succession of human bodies, we naturally make the inquiry: What is this living something, this persistent reincarnating Principle? As our understanding of the whole teaching hinges on our thorough understanding of the answer to this question, it will not be wasted time to dwell a little on the circumstances which led up to and surrounded the first incarnation of this living Principle in the human form. To make this incarnation thoroughly intelligible, we must trace the steps of the evolution of man.

Those who have read the first of these *Manuals* will remember that the Monad or Âtmâ-Buddhi is described as the "mainspring of all evolution, the impelling force

[1] From the translation by Annie Besant, Discourse ii., 18-25.

at the root of all things ".[1] Those to whom the technical name is unfamiliar will seize the idea conveyed by the name to the Theosophist, if they will think of the Universal Life, the Root of all that is, gradually evolving as its own manifestation the various forms which make up our world. We cannot here retrace our earth's story in former stages of its æonian evolution; that will, I hope, be done in one of this series of *Manuals*. But here we must be content to pick up the thread at the beginning of the present stage, when the germ of what was to become man had appeared, as the result of previous evolution, on our globe. H. P. Blavatsky, in the second volume of the *Secret Doctrine*, has drawn the evolution in detail, and to that work I must refer the earnest and thorough student. Let it suffice to say that the physical form of what was to be man was slowly and very gradually evolved, two great Races passing through their full development, and a third Race having run half its course, before humanity had reached completion so far as its physical, or animal, nature was concerned. This nature, rightly called animal, because it contains that which man has in common with the brute—a dense physical body, its etheric double, its vitality, its passions, appetites and desires—this nature was builded up by terrestrial and other cosmic forces through millions of years. It was brooded over, enveloped in, permeated by, that Universal Life which is "the Force back of Evolution," that life which men have in all ages called Divine.

An Occult Commentary, quoted in the *Secret Doctrine*,[2] speaking of this stage of evolution, mentions the forms, technically called "astral doubles," which had evolved

[1] Page 63. [2] Vol. i., 206, new ed.

into the physical bodies of men, and thus describes the situation at the point we have reached: this

Rûpa (Form) has become the vehicle of Monads (Seventh and Sixth Principles) that had completed their cycle of transmigration in the three preceding Kalpas (Rounds). Then they (the astral doubles) became the men of the First Human Race of the Round. But they were not complete, and were senseless.

Here were, we may say, the two poles of the evolving Life-manifestation: the Animal with all its potentialities on the lower plane, but necessarily mindless, conscienceless, errant aimlessly over the earth, unconsciously tending onwards by reason of the impelling force within it that drove it ever forward; this force, the Divine, itself too lofty in its pure ethereal nature to reach consciousness on the lower planes, and so unable to bridge the gulf that stretched between it and the animal brain it vivified but could not illume. Such was the organism that was to become man, a creature of marvellous potentialities, an instrument with strings all ready to break into music; where was the power that should make the potentialities actual, where the touch that should waken the melody and send it forth thrilling into space?

When the hour had struck, the answer came from the mental or mânasic plane. Whilst this double evolution above described, the monadic and the physical, had been going on upon our globe, a third line of evolution, which was to find its goal in man, had been proceeding in a higher sphere. This line was that of intellectual evolution, and the subjects of the evolution are the lower of the Sons of Mind (Mânasaputra), self-conscious intelligent Entities, as is implied by their name. The Mânasaputra are spoken of under many different names:

Lords of Light, Dhyân Chohans, Kumâras, Dragons of Wisdom, Solar Pitris, etc., etc., allegorical and poetical names, that become attractive and familiar to the student in the course of his reading, but which cause much trouble and confusion to the beginner, who cannot make out whether he is dealing with one class of beings or with a dozen. As a matter of fact the name covers many grades. But the one thing that the beginner needs to grasp is that, at a certain stage of evolution, there entered into, incarnated in men, certain self-conscious intelligent Entities, with a long past of intellectual evolution behind them, who found in physical man the instrument ready, and fitted, for their further evolution.

The coming of these Sons of Mind is given in poetical phrase in the Stanzas from the *Book of Dzyan* :—[1]

The Sons of Wisdom, the Sons of Night, ready for rebirth, came down. . . . The Third [*Race*] *were ready. "In these shall we dwell," said the Lords of the Flame. . . . The Third Race became the Vâhan* [*Vehicle*] *of the Lords of Wisdom.*

These Lords of Wisdom incarnated as teachers, and became the fathers of the reincarnating Egos of men, while Solar Pitris of a lower grade became themselves the reincarnating Egos of the leading races; these are the Mind, or rather Minds, in men, the Manas, or Fifth Principle, sometimes described as the Human, or Rational Soul. I prefer to speak of the reincarnating Ego as the *Thinker*, rather than as *Mind*, in man; for the word Thinker suggests an individual Entity, whereas the word Mind suggests a vague generality.

It is interesting and significant that the word *man*, running through so many languages, is related back to

[1] *Secret Doctrine*, ii., 20, 21, new ed.

this Manas, to its root *man*, to think. Skeat[1] gives the word in English, Swedish, Danish, German, Icelandish, Gothic, Latin (*mas*, for *mans*), deriving it from the Sanskrit root *man*, and therefore defining man as a "thinking animal". So that whenever we say Man, we say Thinker, and are carried back to that period at which the Thinkers "came down," *i.e.*, became incarnate in the physical vehicle builded for their reception, when the senseless animal became the thinking being, by virtue of the Manas that entered into him and dwelt in him. It was then that the Man became clothed in his "coat of skin," after his fall into physical matter in order that he might eat of the Tree of Knowledge and thus become a "God".

This man is the link between the Divine and the Animal, that we have viewed as essentially connected and yet held apart from close intercommunion. He stretches one hand upwards towards the Divine Monad, to the Spirit whose offspring he is, striving upwards, that he may assimilate that loftier nature, that his intelligence may become spiritual, his knowledge wisdom; he lays his other hand upon the Animal, which is to bear him to conquest of the lower planes, that he may train and subdue it to his own ends, and make it a perfect instrument for manifestation of the higher life. Long is the task that lies before him; no less than to raise the Animal to the Divine, to sublime Matter into Spirit, to lead up the ascending arc the life that has traversed the descending, and has now to climb upwards, bearing with it all the fruits of its long exile from its true home. Finally he is to reunite the separated aspects of the One, to bring the Spirit to self-consciousness on all planes, Matter to be its perfect manifestation. Such

[1] *Etymological Dictionary*, under "Man".

his sublime task, for the accomplishment of which reincarnation is to be his tool.

This Man, then, is our real Human Self, and we err when we think of our body as "I," and too much exalt our temporary "coat of skin". It is as though a man should regard his coat as himself, himself as a mere appendage of his clothes. As our clothes exist for us and not we for them, and they are only things rendered necessary by climate, comfort and custom, so our bodies are only necessary to us because of the conditions that surround us, and are for our service, not for our subjugation. Some Indians will never speak of bodily wants as theirs: they say, "My body is hungry," "My body is tired"—not "I am hungry," or "I am tired". And though in our ears the phrase may sound fantastic, it is truer to facts than our self-identification with our body. If we were in the habit of identifying ourselves in thought not with the habitation we live in, but with the Human Self that dwells therein, life would become a greater and a serener thing. We should brush off troubles as we brush the dust from our garments, and we should realise that the measure of all things happening to us is not the pain or pleasure they bring to our bodies, but the progress or retardation they bring to the Man within us; and since all things are matters of experience and lessons may be learned from each, we should take the sting out of griefs by searching in each for the wisdom enwrapped in it as the petals are folded within the bud. In the light of reincarnation life changes its aspect, for it becomes the school of the eternal Man within us, who seeks therein his development, the Man that was and is and shall be, for whom the hour will never strike.

Let the beginner, then, get firm grip of the idea that

the Thinker is the Man, the Individual, the reincarnating Ego, and that this Ego seeks to become united to the divine Monad, while training and purifying the animal self to which it is joined during earth-life. United to that divine Monad, a spark of the Universal Life and inseparable from it, the Thinker becomes the Spiritual Ego, the Divine Man.[1] The Thinker is spoken of sometimes as the vehicle of the Monad, the ethereal encasement, as it were, through which the Monad may act on all planes; hence, we often find theosophical writers saying that the Triad, or Trinity, in Man, is that which reincarnates, and the expression, though loose, may pass, if the student remembers that the Monad is Universal, not particular, and that it is only our ignorance which deludes us into separating ourselves from our brothers, and seeing any difference between the Light in one and the Light in another.[2] The Monad being Universal, and not differing in different persons or individuals, it is really only the Thinker that can in strictness be said to reincarnate, and it is with this Thinker, as the Individual, that we are concerned.

Now in this Thinker reside all the powers that we class as Mind. In it are memory, intuition, will. It gathers up all the experiences of the earth-lives through which it passes, and stores these accumulated treasures of knowledge, to be transmuted within itself, by its own divine alchemy, into that essence of experience and knowledge which is Wisdom. Even in our brief span of earth-life we distinguish between the knowledge we

[1] *The Seven Principles of Man*, by Annie Besant, p. 60.

[2] *Ibid.*, p. 68. The relation between the three Higher Principles is clearly explained in this little book, which appeared originally in *Lucifer* as a series of articles, and is supposed to have been studied by the readers of the present manual.

acquire and the wisdom we gradually—alas! too rarely—distil from that knowledge. Wisdom is the fruitage of a life's experience, the crowning possession of the aged. And in a much fuller and richer sense, Wisdom is the fruitage of many incarnations, in which knowledge has been gained, experience garnered, patience has had her perfect work, so that at length the divine Man is the glorious product of the centuried evolution. In the Thinker, then, is our store of experiences, reaped in all past lives, harvested through many rebirths, a heritage into which each one shall surely come when he learns to rise above the thrall of the senses, out of the storm and stress of earthly life, to that purer region, to that higher plane, where our true Self resides.

What it is that does NOT Reincarnate.

We have seen, in the preceding Section, that man's outer form, his physical nature, was built up slowly, through two and a half Races, until it was ready to receive the Son of Mind.[1] This is the nature we have called animal, and it consists of four distinguishable parts or "principles": I., the body; II., the etheric double; III., the vitality; IV., the passional nature—passions, appetites and desires. This is, in very truth, the animal-man, differing from its relatives which are purely animal by the influence exerted over it by the Thinker, who has come to train and ennoble it. Take away the Thinker, as in the case of the congenital idiot, and you have an animal merely, albeit its form be human.

Now the Thinker, connected with and informing the animal-man, imparts to this lower nature such of its own

[1] See *ante*, pp. 10, 11.

capacities as that animal-man is able to manifest, and these capacities, working in and through the human brain, are recognised by us as the brain-mind, or the lower mind. In the West the development of this brain-mind is regarded as marking the distinction, in ordinary parlance, between the brute and the human being. That which the Theosophist looks on as merely the lower or brain-mind, is considered by the average Western to be the mind itself, and hence arises much confusion when the Theosophist and the non-Theosophist foregather. We say that the Thinker, striving to reach and influence the animal-man, sends out a Ray that plays on and in the brain, and that through the brain are manifested so much of the mental powers as that brain, by its configuration and other physical qualities, is able to translate. This Ray sets the molecules of the brain nerve-cells vibrating, as a ray of light sets quivering the molecules of the retinal nerve-cells, and so gives rise to consciousness on the physical plane. Reason, judgment, memory, will, ideation—as these faculties are known to us, manifested when the brain is in full activity—all these are the outcome of the Ray sent forth by the Thinker, modified by the material conditions through which it must work. These conditions include healthy nerve-cells, properly balanced development of the respective groups of nerve-cells, a full supply of blood containing nutritive matter that can be assimilated by the cells so as to supply waste, and carrying oxygen easily set free from its vehicles. If these conditions, or any of them, are absent, the brain cannot function, and thought processes can no more be carried out through such a brain than a melody can be produced from an organ the bellows of which is broken. The brain no more produces the thought than the organ produces the melody; in both cases there is a player working through the instrument. But the power of the player to manifest himself, in thought or in melody, is limited by the capacities of the instrument.

It is absolutely necessary that the student should clearly appreciate this difference between the Thinker and the animal-man whose brain is played on by the Thinker, for any confusion between the two will render unintelligible the doctrine of reincarnation. For while the Thinker reincarnates, *the animal-man does not*.

Here is really the difficulty which leads to so many other difficulties. The animal-man is born, and the true Man is linked to him; through the brain of the animal-man the true Man works, incarnation after incarnation, and remains one. It informs in turn the animal-men Sashital Dev, Caius Glabrio, Johanna Wirther, William Johnson—let us say—and in each reaps experience, through each gathers knowledge, from each takes the material it supplies, and weaves it into its own eternal Being. The animal-man wins his immortality by union with his true Self; Sashital Dev does not reincarnate as Caius Glabrio, and then as Johanna Wirther, blossoming out as William Johnson in nineteenth century England, but it is the one eternal Son of Mind that dwells in each of these in turn, gathering up from each such indwelling new experience, fresh knowledge. It is this reincarnating Ego alone that can look back along the line of its rebirths, remembering each earthly life, the story of each pilgrimage from cradle to grave, the whole drama unrolled act by act, century after century. Taking my imaginary actors, William Johnson in the nineteenth century cannot look back on, nor remember, *his* rebirths, for *he* has never been born before, nor have *his* eyes seen the light of an earlier day. But the innate character of William Johnson, the character with which he came into the world, is the character wrought and hammered out by Johanna Wirther in Germany, Caius Glabrio in Rome, Sashital Dev in Hindustan, and by many another of his earthly predecessors in many lands and under many civilisations; he is adding new touches to this work of the ages by his daily life, so that it will pass from his hands different from what it was, baser or nobler, into the hands of his heir and successor on the life-stage, who is thus, in a very real but not external sense, himself.

Thus the question which arises so naturally in the mind, and which is so often asked: "Why do I not remember my past lives?" is really based on a misconception of the theory of reincarnation. "I," the true "I," does remember; but the animal-man, not yet in full responsive union with his true Self, cannot remember a past in which he, personally, had no share. Brain-memory can contain only a record of the events in which the brain has been concerned, and the brain of the present William Johnson is not the brain of Johanna Wirther, nor that of Caius Glabrio, nor that of Sashital Dev. William Johnson can only obtain memory of the past lives linked with his, by his brain becoming able to vibrate in answer to the subtle delicate vibrations sent down to it through that Ray which is the bridge between his transient personal self and his eternal SELF. To do this he must be closely united to that real Self, and must be living in the consciousness that *he* is not William Johnson but that Son of Mind, and that William Johnson is only the temporary house in which he is living for his own purposes. Instead of living in the brain-consciousness, he must live in the higher consciousness; instead of thinking of his true Self as without, as something outside, and of the transitory William Johnson as "I," he must identify himself with the Thinker, and look on William Johnson as the external organ, useful for work on the material plane, and to be educated and trained up to the highest point of efficiency, that efficiency including the quick responsiveness of the William Johnson brain to its real owner.

As this difficult opening of the man of flesh to influences from the higher planes is gradually carried on, and as the true Self is increasingly able to affect its bodily habitation, glimpses of past incarnations will flash on the lower consciousness, and these will become less like flashes and more like permanent visions, until finally the past is recognised as "mine" by the continuous thread of memory that gives the feeling of individuality. Then the present incarnation is recognised as being merely the last garment in which the Self has clothed itself, and it is in no wise identified with that Self, any more than a coat which a man puts on is regarded by him as being part of himself. A man does not regard his coat as part of himself, because he is consciously able to put it off and look at it separated from himself. When the true Man does that with his body, consciously on this plane, certainty becomes complete.

The coat then—the "coat of skin," the etheric double, the vitality, the passional nature—does not reincarnate, but its elements disintegrate, and return to those to which they belong in the lower worlds. All that was best in William Johnson passes on with the Ego into a period of blissful rest, until the impulse that carried it out of earth-life is exhausted, and it falls back to earth.

The Method of Reincarnation.

Having now gained a clear idea of the reincarnating Ego, or Thinker, and of the distinction between it and the transitory animal-man, the student must address himself to the understanding of the method of Reincarnation.

This method will be best appreciated by considering the plane to which the Thinker belongs, and the Force wherewith it works. The Thinker is what is called the Fifth Principle in man; and this Fifth Principle in the microcosm, man, answers to the Fifth Plane of the macrocosm, the universe outside man. These planes are differentiations of primary Substance, according to the Esoteric Philosophy, and consciousness works on each plane through the conditions, whatever they may be, of each plane. *Substance* is a word used to express Existence in its earliest objective form, the primary manifestation of the periodical aspect of the ONE, the first film of the future Kosmos, in the dim beginnings of all manifested things. This Substance has in it the potentiality of all, of most ethereal Spirit, of densest Matter. As Sir W. Crookes in chemistry posits a protyle, or a first substance, out of which atoms are built up, and out of atoms molecules, and out of molecules compound substances, and so on in ever-increasing complexity —so the Esoteric Philosophy posits a primary Substance, out of which Kosmos is evolved, which at its rarest is Spirit, Energy, Force, and at its densest the most solid Matter, every varying form in all worlds being of this Substance, aggregated into more or less dense masses, instinct with more or less Force. A plane only means a stage of existence in which this Spirit-Matter varies within certain limits, and acts under certain "laws". Thus the physical plane means our visible, audible, tangible, odorous, gustable world, in which we come into contact with Spirit-Matter—Science calls it Force *and* Matter, as though separable—by way of the senses, whether it be as solid, liquid, gas, etc. And so on with other planes, each being distinguishable by the characteristics of its Spirit-Matter. On each of these planes consciousness shows itself, working through the Spirit-Matter of the plane. One further fact must be added to this rough and very condensed statement, that these planes are not, as has been said, like skins of an onion, one over the other, but, like the air and the ether in our bodies, they interpenetrate each other.

Answering to these are seven principles, which bear relation by analogy to the seven planes in Kosmos. Of these the Thinker is the Fifth.

Now this fifth principle in man corresponds to the fifth plane in Kosmos, that of Mahat, the Universal Mind, Divine Ideation, from which proceeds directly the moulding, guiding, directing Force, which is the essence of all the differentiations that we call forces on the physical plane. [This plane is often called the third, because starting from Âtmâ as the first, it is the third. It does not matter by what number it is called, if the student understands what it is in relation to the rest.] All the world of form, be the form subtle or dense, is evolved by and through this Force of the Universal Mind, aggregating and separating the atoms, integrating them into forms, disintegrating them again, building up and pulling down, constructing and destroying, attracting and repelling. One Force to the eye of the philosopher, many forces to the observation of the scientist, verily one in its essence and manifold in its manifestations. Thus from the fifth plane come all the creations of forms, using creation in the sense of moulding pre-existent material, fashioning it into new forms. This Thought Force is, in the Esoteric Philosophy, the one source of form; it is spoken of by H. P. Blavatsky, as

The mysterious power of thought which enables it to produce external, perceptible, phenomenal results by its own inherent energy.[1]

As in the fifth plane of Kosmos, so in the fifth principle of man; in the Thinker lies the Force by which all things are made, and it is in this creative power of thought that we shall find the secret of the method of reincarnation.

Those who desire to prove to themselves that thought gives rise to images, to "thought-forms," so that in most literal truth "a thought is a thing," may find what they seek in the records now so widely scattered of so-called hypnotic experiments. The thought-form of an idea may be projected on a blank paper, and there become visible to a hypnotised person: or it may be made so objective that the hypnotised person will see and feel it as though it were an actual physical object. Again, a "medium" will see as a "spirit" a thought of a human being in the mind of a person present, this thought being imaged in his aura, the magnetic atmosphere that surrounds him. Or a clairvoyant, entranced or awake, will recognise and describe an image deliberately formed by a person present, no word being spoken, but the will being exercised to outline the image clearly in thought. All persons who "visualise" much are to some extent clairvoyant, and may prove to themselves by personal experiment this power to mould subtle matter by the will.

The less subtle astral matter, again, may be thus moulded, as H. P. Blavatsky, at the Eddy farmhouse, moulded the projected astral image of the medium into likenesses of persons known to herself and unknown to the others present. Nor can this be considered strange when we remember how habits of thought mould even

[1] *Secret Doctrine*, i., 312, new ed.

the dense matter of which our physical bodies are composed, until the character of the aged becomes stamped on the face, their beauty consisting not in form and colouring but in expression—expression, which is the mask moulded on the inner self. Any habitual line of thought, vice or virtue, makes its impress on the physical features, and we do not need clairvoyant eyes to scan the aura to tell if the mental attitude be generous or grasping, trustful or suspicious, loving or hating. This is a fact so common that it makes on us no impression, and yet it is significant enough; for if the dense matter of the body be thus moulded by the forces of thought, what is there of incredible, or even of strange, in the idea that the subtler forms of matter should be equally plastic, and should submissively take the shapes into which they are moulded by the deft fingers of the immortal Artist, thinking Man?

The position, then, that is here taken is that Manas, in its inherent nature, is a form-producing energy, and that the succession of events in the manifestation of an external object is: Manas puts forth a thought, and this thought takes form on the mânasic or mind world; it passes out into the kâma-mânasic, there becoming denser; thence to the astral, where, being yet denser, it is visible to the eye of the clairvoyant; if directed consciously by a trained will, it may pass at once to the physical plane, and be there clothed in physical matter, thus becoming objective to ordinary eyes, whereas, in ordinary cases, it remains on the astral plane, as a mould which will be built into objective life when circumstances occur which draw it thitherwards. A Master has written of the Adept being able

To project into and materialise in the visible world the forms that his imagination has constructed out of inert

cosmic matter in the invisible world. The Adept does not create anything new, but only utilises and manipulates materials which Nature has in store around him, and material which, throughout eternities, has passed through all the forms. He has but to choose the one he wants, and recall it into objective existence.[1]

A reference to well-known facts on the physical plane may perhaps help the reader to realise how the invisible may thus become the visible; I have spoken of a form gradually densifying as it passes from the mânasic to the kâma-mânasic world, from the latter to the astral, from the astral to the physical. Think of a glass receiver, apparently empty, but in reality filled with the invisible gases, hydrogen and oxygen; a spark causes combination and "water" exists there, but in a state of gas; the receiver is cooled, and gradually a steamy vapour becomes visible; then the vapour condenses on the glass as drops of water; then the water congeals and becomes a film of solid ice crystals. So when the mânasic spark flashes out it combines subtle matter into a thought-form; this densifies into the kâma-mânasic form—our analogy is the steamy vapour; this into the astral—our analogy is the water; and so into the physical—for which the ice may stand. The student of the Esoteric Philosophy will know that in the evolution of Nature all proceeds in orderly sequence, and he will be accustomed to see in the sub-states of matter on the physical plane analogies to its states on the different planes of the "invisible" worlds. But for the non-Theosophist, the illustration is offered only by way of giving a concrete physical picture of the densifying process, showing how the invisible may condense itself into the visible.

[1] *The Occult World*, 5th ed., p. 88.

In truth, however, this process of condensation of rarer into grosser matter is of the commonest facts of our experience. The vegetable world grows by taking in gases from the atmosphere, and transforming their materials into solids and liquids. The activity of the vital force shows itself by this constant building up of visible forms out of invisible; and whether the thought-process named be true or not, there is nothing in it inherently impossible or even extraordinary. Its truth is a matter of evidence, and here the evidence of those who can see the thought-forms on the different planes is surely more valuable than the evidence of those who cannot. The word of a hundred blind men denying a visible object is of less weight than the word of one man who can see and who testifies to his seeing of it. In this matter the Theosophist may be content to wait, knowing that facts do not alter for denials, and that the world will gradually come round to a knowledge of the existence of thought-forms, as it has already come round—after a similar period of scoffing—to a knowledge of the existence of some of the facts asserted by Mesmer at the close of the last century.

It has been found, then, that events take their rise on the mânasic or kâma-mânasic plane, as ideas, or as thoughts of passion or emotion, etc.; they then take astral form, and lastly appear objectively on the physical plane as acts or events, so that the latter are effects of pre-existing mental causes. Now the body is such an effect, according to the Esoteric Philosophy, and it is moulded on the etheric double, a term which will, by this time, be sufficiently familiar to my readers. The idea must be clearly grasped of a body of etheric matter, serving as a mould into which denser matter may be built, and if the method of reincarnation is to be at all understood, this conception of the dense body as the result of the building of dense molecules into a pre-existing etheric mould must, for the moment, be accepted.

And now let us return to the idea of the Thinker, creating forms, working certainly through the lower manas, or kâma manas, in the average man, since of purely mânasic activity we may not hope to find yet awhile many traces. In our daily life we think and thus create thought-forms:—

Man is continually peopling his current in space with a world of his own, crowded with the offspring of his fancies, desires, impulses and passions.[1]

[The consideration of the effect of this on others belongs to the subject of Karma, to be hereafter dealt with.] These thought-forms remain in his aura, or magnetic atmosphere, and as time goes on their increased number acts on him with ever-gathering force, repetition of thoughts and of types of thought adding to their intensity day by day, with cumulative energy, until certain kinds of thought-forms so dominate his mental life that the man rather answers to their impulse than decides anew, and what we call a habit, the outer reflection of this stored-up force, is set up. Thus "character" is built, and if we are intimately acquainted with any one of mature character, we are able to predicate with tolerable certainty his action in any given set of circumstances.

When the death hour comes the subtler bodies free themselves from the physical, the etheric double disintegrating gradually with the dense frame. The thought-body resulting from the past life persists for a considerable time and goes through various processes of consolidation of experiences, assimilation of much differentiated thoughts, and, handing on its results to the causal body, it in turn

[1] A MASTER in *The Occult World*, p. 90.

disintegrates. As the period for reincarnation approaches the causal body, or reincarnating Ego, builds a new mental and a new astral body, while the Lords of Karma provide a mould suited to express the Karma to be worked out, and after this the etheric double is built. Since the brain, in common with the rest of the dense body, is built into this etheric double, this brain is, by its conformation, the physical expression, however imperfect, of the mental habits and qualities of the human being then to be incarnated, the fitting physical vehicle for the exercise of the capacities which his experience now enables him to manifest on the physical plane.

Let us, as an example, take the case of the practice of a vicious and of a virtuous type of thought, say of a selfish and of an unselfish character. One person continually gives birth to thought-forms of selfishness, desires for self, hopes for self, plans for self, and these forms clustering round him react again upon him, and he tends to become unscrupulous in his self-service, disregarding the claims of others, and seeking but his own ends. He dies, and his character has hardened into the selfish type. This persists, and in due course is given etheric form, as mould for the next dense body. Drawn towards a family of similar type, towards parents physically able to supply materials stamped with similar characteristics, the dense body is built into this etheric mould, and the brain takes the shape physically fitted for the manifestation of the brute tendencies to self-gratification, with a corresponding lack of the physical basis for the manifestation of the social virtues. In an extreme case of persistent and unscrupulous selfishness during one incarnation, we have the cause of the building of the "criminal type of brain" for the succeeding one, and the child comes into the world with this instrument of miserable quality, from which the Immortal Thinker will be able to draw scarce a note of pure and tender melody, strive he as he may. All the life through the Ray of Manas incarnated in this personality will be dimmed, broken, struggling through kâmic clouds. Sometimes, despite all opposing circumstances, the glorious radiant quality will illume and transform to some extent its physical vehicle, and with anguish and effort the lower nature will now and again be trampled under foot, and, however slowly, a painful step or two of progress will be achieved. But all the life through, the past will dominate the present, and the cup filled in forgotten days must be drained to the last drop by the quivering lips.

In the second supposed case, a person continually gives birth to thought-forms of unselfishness, helpful desires for others, loving plans for the welfare of others, earnest hopes for the good of others. These cluster round him and react on him, and he tends to become habitually selfless, habitually placing the welfare of others before his own, and so, when he dies, his character has become ingrainedly unselfish. Coming back to earth-life, the model form which represents his previous characteristics is drawn to a family fitted to supply materials of a pure kind, habituated to respond to the promptings of the Higher Man. These, builded into the etheric mould, yield a brain physically fitted for the manifestation of the self-sacrificing tendencies, and a corresponding lack of the physical basis for the manifestation of the brute instincts. So here, in an extreme case of self-sacrificing habit through one incarnation, we have the cause of the building of the benevolent and philanthropic type of brain for the succeeding one, and the child comes into the world with this instrument of splendid quality, which thrills beneath the lightest touch of the Immortal Thinker, breathing forth divine melodies of love and service, till the world wonders at the glory of a human life, at results that seem the mere outflow of the nature rather than the crown of effort deliberately made. But these royal natures that overflow in blessing are the outer symbol of long conflicts gallantly waged, of conflicts of a past unknown to the present, but known to the inner Conqueror, and one day to be known to the personality he informs.

Thus step by step is brought about the evolution of man, character being moulded in personality after personality, gains and losses rigidly recorded in astral and mental forms, and these governing the succeeding physical manifestations. Every virtue is thus the outer sign and symbol of a step forward made, of repeated victories won over the lower nature, and the "innate quality," the mental or moral characteristic with which a child is born, is the indubitable proof of past struggles, of past triumphs, or of past failures. A distasteful doctrine enough to the morally or mentally slothful and cowardly, but a most cheering and enheartening teaching for those who do not ask to be pensioners on any charity, human or divine, but are content to earn patiently and laboriously all they claim to own.

Very nobly has Edward Carpenter put this truth in *Towards Democracy*, in the "Secret of Time and Satan".

> The art of creation, like every other art, has to be learned;
> Slowly, slowly, through many years, thou buildest up thy body.
> And the power that thou now hast (such as it is) to build up this present body, thou hast acquired in the past in other bodies;
> So in the future shalt thou use again the power that thou now acquirest.
> But the power to build up the body includes all powers.
>
> . . . .
>
> Beware how thou seekest this for thyself and that for thyself. I do not say, Seek not; but, Beware how thou seekest.

For a soldier who is going a campaign does not seek what fresh furniture he can carry on his back, but rather what he may leave behind;

Knowing well that every additional thing which he cannot freely use and handle is an impediment to him.

So if thou seekest fame, or ease, or pleasure, or aught for thyself, the image of that thing which thou seekest will come and cling to thee—and thou wilt have to carry it about—

And the images and powers which thou hast thus evoked will gather round and form for thee a new body—clamouring for sustenance and satisfaction.

And if thou art not able to discard this image now, thou wilt not be able to discard that body then; but wilt have to carry it about.

Beware then lest it become thy grave and thy prison—instead of thy winged abode and palace of joy.

. . . .

And seest thou not that except for Death thou couldst never overcome Death?

For since by being a slave to things of sense thou hast clothed thyself with a body which thou art not master of, thou wert condemned to a living tomb were that body not to be destroyed. But now through pain and suffering out of this tomb shalt thou come; and through the experience thou hast acquired shalt build thyself a new and better body;

And so on many times, till thou spreadest wings and hast all powers diabolic and angelic concentred in thy flesh.

. . . .

And the bodies which I took on yielded before him, and were like cinctures of flame upon me, but I flung them aside;

And the pains which I endured in one body were powers which I wielded in the next.

Great truths, greatly spoken. And one day men will believe them in the West, as they believe them, and have ever believed them, in the East.

Through thousands of generations the Immortal Thinker thus patiently toils at his mission of leading the animal-man upwards till he is fit to become one with the Divine. Out of a life, he wins perchance but a mere fragment for his work, yet the final model is of type a little less animal than the man, whose life-work is therein embodied, was when he came into earth-life. On that slightly improved model will be moulded the next man, and from him, at death, is obtained a mould which is again a little less animal, to serve for the next physical body, and so on and on, again and again, generation after generation, millennium after millennium; with many retrogressions constantly recovered; with many failures gallantly made good; with many wounds slowly healed; yet on the whole, upward; yet on the whole, forward; the animal lessening, the human increasing; such is the story of human evolution, such the slowly accomplished task of the Ego, as he raises himself to divine manhood. At a stage in this progress the personalities begin to become translucent, to answer to the vibrations from the Thinker, and dimly to sense that they are something more than isolated lives, are attached to something permanent, immortal. They may not quite recognise their goal, but they begin to thrill and quiver under the touch of the Light, as buds quiver in the springtime within their cases, preparing to burst them open and to expand in the sunshine. This sense of inborn eternity, and of wondering as to the end, comes out strongly in one of Walt Whitman's poems:—

Facing West from California's shores,
Inquiring, tireless, seeking what is yet unfound,
I a child, very old, over waves, towards the house of maternity, the land of migrations, look afar,
Look off the shores of my Western sea, the circle almost circled;
For starting westward from Hindûstân, from the vales of Kashmere,
From Asia, from the north, from the God, the sage, and the hero,
From the south, from the flowery peninsulas and the spice islands,

Long having wandered since, round the earth having wandered,
Now I face home again, very pleased and joyous.
(But where is what I started for so long ago?
And why is it yet unfound?)

The Object of Reincarnation.

We have already seen generally that the object of reincarnation is to train the animal-man until it becomes the perfect instrument of the Divine, and that the agent in this training is the reincarnating Ego. Let us briefly trace the road by which this goal is reached.

When the Mânasaputra come down to ensoul the animal-man, their habitation is of matter that has not yet reached its maximum of density. The Thinker, working through this, produces at first what are called psychic qualities in contradistinction to intellectual; the spiritual, on its first contact with astral matter, translates itself into the psychic, and only gradually becomes intellectual, *i.e.*, logical, reasoning, deliberative, by prolonged contact with matter of the denser type. At first intuitive, clairvoyant, communicating with its fellows by thought-transference, as it has to work with denser materials and throw their heavier particles into vibrations, intuition is transformed into reasoning and thought-transference into language. The process is best realised by conceiving of vibrations being set up in ever denser and denser matter, the vibrations in the less dense translating themselves as psychic, in the more dense as rational, qualities. The psychic are the swifter, subtler, more direct, faculties, including clairvoyance, clairaudience, lower forms of intuition, power to transmit and receive thought-impressions without speech; the rational are slower, and include all the processes of the brain-mind, their characteristic being deliberative reasoning, the forging of a logical chain, hammering it out link by link, and, as a necessary condition of this mental labour, the elaboration of language. When this process has been perfected, and the brain has reached its highest point of intellection, responding swiftly to the astral impulses as they reach it, and at once translating them into their intellectual analogues, then the time has come for the next great step onwards, the training of the brain to respond directly to the subtler vibrations, and take them into brain-consciousness without the delaying process of translation. Then the exercise of psychic faculties becomes part of the conscious equipment of the developing man, and they are employed normally and without effort or strain, the brain-mind and the psyche thus becoming unified, and all psychic powers regained with the addition of the intellectual experience. The temporary obscuration, due to the accretion of the densest matter round the developing man, gradually diminishes as the matter grows ductile and translucent, and thus gross matter is "redeemed," *i.e.*, trained into a perfect vehicle of manifestation for spirit. "Civilisation has ever developed the physical and the intellectual at the cost of the psychic and spiritual,"[1] but without this development animal-man could not become divine, the "perfect septenary being" whom it is the object of reincarnation to evolve.

In our own Aryan Race we are on the ascending arc; intellectuality pure and simple is reaching its highest possibilities, and on all sides are appearing signs of psychic activities, which, when developed *beyond* the intellect and not behind it, are the marks of the commencing triumph of the spiritual Man. In some men of our race this

[1] *Secret Doctrine*, ii., 332, new ed.

triumph has been consummated, and these are they who are spoken of as Arhats, Mahâtmas, and Masters. With Them the body is the mere vehicle of the spiritual Man, who is no longer cabined and confined by the body he inhabits, but for whom the body is the convenient instrument for work on the physical plane, obediently answering every impulse of its owner, and placing at his disposal powers and faculties for use in the world of gross matter otherwise unattainable by a spiritual Being. A Spirit may be active on the spiritual plane, but is senseless on all others, being unable to act by its subtle essence on planes of grosser matter. A spiritual Intelligence may be active on the spiritual and mental planes, but is still too subtle to work on the grosser. Only as by incarnation it conquers matter through matter, can it become active on all planes, the "perfect septenary being". This is the meaning of Arhatship; the Arhat is the spiritual Intelligence that has conquered, subdued, and trained matter, until his body is but the materialised expression of himself, and he is ready for the step that makes him "Master," or the Christ triumphant.

Naturally, in such a perfected septenary being are gathered up all the forces of the universe, spiritual, psychic and material. As man's living body has in it in miniature the forces found in the physical universe, so, as the psychic and spiritual natures make their impulses felt, the forces of the psychic and spiritual universes can be brought to bear upon the physical. Hence the apparently "miraculous," the bringing about of effects the causes of which are hidden, but which are not therefore non-existent; just as the closing of a galvanic circuit may bring about an explosion many miles from the point of closure, so may the action of the trained will manifest itself in material phenomena on a plane far beneath its own.

Man's ignorance makes the supernatural; knowledge reduces all to the natural; for Nature is but one aspect of the ALL, that aspect which, at the time, is in manifestation.

The question may here arise: And this object attained, what end is thereby served? At this point, several Paths stretch before the triumphant spiritual Man. He has touched the summit of attainment possible here in this world; for further progress he must pass on to other spheres of being; Nirvâna lies open before him, the fulness of spiritual knowledge, the Beatific Vision of which Christians have whispered, the peace which passeth understanding. One Path, the Path of Renunciation, the voluntary acceptance of life on earth for the sake of service to the race, is the Path of which Kwanyin said when setting resolute foot thereon:—

> Never will I seek, nor receive, private individual salvation—never enter into final peace alone; but for ever, and everywhere, will I live and strive for the universal redemption of every creature throughout the world.[1]

The nature and purpose of this choice has been told in the *Book of the Golden Precepts,* fragments from which have been done into such noble English by H. P. Blavatsky. The conqueror stands triumphant; "his mind, like a becalmed and boundless ocean, spreadeth out in shoreless space. He holdeth life and death in his strong hand." Then the question comes:—

> *Now*, he shall surely reach his great reward! Shall he not use the gifts which it confers for his own rest and bliss, his well-earned weal and glory—he, the subduer of the great Delusion?

But the answer rings clearly out:—

> Nay, O thou candidate for Nature's hidden lore! If one would

[1] Quoted in Moncure D. Conway's *Sacred Anthology*, p. 233.

follow in the steps of holy Tathâgata, those gifts and powers are not for self. . . . Know that the stream of superhuman knowledge, and the Deva-Wisdom thou hast won, must, from thyself, the channel of Alâya, be poured forth into another bed. Know, O Narjol, thou of the Secret Path, its pure fresh waters must be used to sweeter make the Ocean's bitter waves—that mighty sea of sorrow, formed of the tears of men. Self-doomed to live through future Kalpas, unthanked and unperceived by man; wedged as a stone with countless other stones which form the "Guardian Wall," such is thy future if the seventh gate thou passest. Built by the hands of many Masters of Compassion, raised by their tortures, by their blood cemented, it shields mankind, since man is man, protecting it from further and far greater misery and sorrow. . . . Compassion speaks and saith: "Can there be bliss when all that lives must suffer? Shalt thou be saved and hear the whole world cry?" Now thou hast heard that which was said. Thou shalt attain the seventh step and cross the gate of final knowledge but only to wed woe—if thou wouldst be Tathâgata, follow upon thy predecessor's steps, remain unselfish till the endless end. Thou art enlightened—choose thy way.[1]

The choice which accepts incarnation till the Race has reached its consummation is the crown of the Master, of the perfected man. His wisdom, His powers, all are thrown at the feet of Humanity, to serve it, help it, guide it on the path Himself has trodden. This then is the end that lies beyond reincarnation for Those whose strong souls can make the GREAT RENUNCIATION; They become the Saviours of the world, the blossom and the glory of Their race. Reincarnation builds up the perfect septenary being, and his individual triumph subserves the redemption of Humanity as a whole.

THE CAUSES OF REINCARNATION.

The fundamental cause of Reincarnation, as of all manifestation, is the desire for active life, the thirst for

[1] *Voice of the Silence*, pp. 65-68, 71.

sentient existence. Some deep-lying essence of nature, obvious in its workings, but incomprehensible as to its origin and reason, manifests as the "law of periodicity". "An alternation such as that of Day and Night, Life and Death, Sleeping and Waking, is a fact so common, so perfectly universal and without exception, that it is easy to comprehend that in it we see one of the absolutely fundamental laws of the universe."[1] The ebb and flow everywhere, the rhythm which is the systole and diastole of the kosmic Heart, is manifest on every hand. But the reason for it escapes us; we cannot say why things should be so; we can only see that so they are. And in the Esoteric Philosophy this same law is recognised as extending to the emanation and reabsorption of universes, the Night and Day of Brahmâ, the outbreathing and the inbreathing of the Great Breath.

Hence the Hindus have pictured the God of Desire as the impulse to manifestation. "Kâma, again, is in the *Rig Veda* (x., 129) the personification of that feeling which leads and propels to creation. He was the *first movement* that stirred the ONE, after its manifestation from the purely abstract Principle, to create. 'Desire first arose in It, which was the primal germ of mind; and which sages, searching with their intellect, have discovered to be the bond which connects Entity with Non-Entity.'"[2] Kâma is, essentially, the longing for active sentient existence, existence of vivid sensation, tossing turbulence of passionate life. When spiritual Intelligence comes into contact with this thirst for sensation, its first action is to intensify it. Says the Stanza: "*From their own essence they filled* (intensified) *the Kâma*".[3] Thus Kâma, for the

[1] *Secret Doctrine*, i., 45, new ed.

[2] *Ibid.*, ii., 185, new ed.

[3] *Ibid.*, 170.

individual as for the Kosmos, becomes the primary cause of reincarnation, and, as Desire differentiates into desires, these chain down the Thinker to earth and bring him back, time after time, to rebirth. The Hindu and Buddhist Scriptures are filled with reiterations of this truth. Thus in the *Bhagavad Gîtâ* we read:—

He whose Buddhi is everywhere unattached, the self subdued, dead to desires, he goeth by renunciation to the supreme perfection of freedom from Karma.[1]

So in the *Udânavarga*, a Northern Buddhist version of the *Dhammapada*, translated from the Tibetan, the same note is struck:—

It is hard for one who is held by the fetters of desire to free himself of them, says the Blessed One. The steadfast, who care not for the happiness of desires, cast them off, and do soon depart (to Nirvâna).[2]

Again and again seeking for it (existence) they again and again enter the womb; beings come and go; to one state of being succeeds another. It is hard to cast off (existence) in this world; he who has cast off lust, who has pulled up the seed (of existence), will no more be subject to transmigration, for he has put an end to lust.[3]

In the Scriptures of the Southern Buddhist Church stress is continually laid on the same idea. The disciple is bidden not to be confident till he has "attained the extinction of desires," and after describing the way in which desires and passions tie men to earthly life, the *Dhammapada* proceeds:—

He who has reached the consummation, who does not tremble, who is without thirst and without sin, he has broken all the thorns of life: this will be his last body. He who is without thirst and

[1] Discourse xviii., 49. [2] Trans. by W. W. Rockhill, p. 10.
[3] *Ibid.*, p. 15.

without affection, who understands the words and their interpretation, who knows the order of letters (those which are before and which are after), he has received his last body, he is called the great sage, the great man. "I have conquered all, I know all, in all conditions of life I am free from taint; I have left all, and through the destruction of thirst I am free."[1]

And so there is the triumphant apostrophe, when Gautama attains Buddhahood:—

Looking for the maker of this tabernacle, I shall have to run through a course of many births, so long as I do not find (him); and painful is birth again and again. But now, maker of the tabernacle, thou hast been seen; thou shalt not make up this tabernacle again. All thy rafters are broken, thy ridge-pole is sundered; the mind, approaching the Eternal, has attained to the extinction of all desires.[2]

When the nature of desire is realised by the student, he will understand why its destruction is necessary to the perfecting of the spiritual Man. Desire must be, till the harvest of experience has been gathered, for only by feeding on that harvested experience can growth be nourished and sustained. So while experience still is lacking, the thirst for it remains unslaked, and the Ego will return to earth again and again. But its fetters must fall off one by one as the Ego reaches the perfecting of its tabernacle, for *desire is personal and therefore selfish*, and when desire prompts action the purity of the action is tainted. The condition of Arhatship is unceasing activity without any personal returns; the Arhat must "give light to all, but take from none".[3] Hence in the upward climbing, one desire after another must be unloosed, desire for personal enjoyment, personal pleasure, personal gain, personal loves, personal attainments,

[1] Chap. xxiv., 351-353. [2] Chap. xi., 153, 154.

[3] *Voice of the Silence*, p. 67.

and, last and subtlest of all, desire for personal perfection, for the personal self must be lost in the ONE SELF, that is the SELF of all that lives.

And here two warnings against misunderstanding are necessary. First: personal loves are not to be killed out, but are to be expanded till they become universal; we are not to love our dearest less, but all are to become dear, so that the sorrow of any child of man shall wring our hearts as much as that of our own child, and stir us into equal activity of help. Loves are to be levelled up, not down. The heart is not to be frozen, but to be aflame for all. The failure to realise this, and the tremendous difficulty of the task, when realised, have led to the stifling of love instead of its growth. Overflowing love, not lovelessness, will save the world. The Mahâtma is the Ocean of Compassion; He is not an iceberg.

It is easy to see why this widening out must precede the attainment of Mastership, for the Master holds His powers for the good of all, and not for the elevation of any particular family or nation. He is the Servant of Humanity, and the way to His help must be need, not kinship. To superhuman powers He must needs join superhuman impartiality, and personal affection must never be allowed to weight the scale of Justice. Beyond all other men He must be a slave to duty, for any swaying from its line would bring about results proportionate to the greatness of His height. He is to be a force for good, and the good must flow in the channels where it is most needed, not in those cut by personal loves or racial predilections. Hence the long training, the personal asceticism, the isolation, which are the conditions of chelaship.

Second: action is not to be stopped because the disciple no longer seeks the fruits of action as reward. "Inaction in a deed of mercy becomes an action in a deadly sin."[1] "Shalt thou abstain from action? Not so shall gain thy soul her freedom. To reach Nirvâna one must reach Self-Knowledge, and Self-Knowledge is of loving deeds the child."[2] But while action must be carried on at the full strain of human powers, desire for its fruit in personal satisfaction must pass away. A good deed must be done for the sake of its helpfulness, of its use to others, not for the sake of praise either of others or of self, nor even for the subtler longing for self-improvement. Here again the failure to realise the distinction between action and desire for the fruits of action has led to the stagnation and passivity characteristic of Eastern nations, since spiritual selfishness and indifference brought on their decay.

As this general desire for sentient existence is the cause of reincarnation universally, so is the determining cause of each individual reincarnation the renewed longing for the taste of existence on the physical plane. When a long life on the earth plane has been lived and a store of experiences has been gathered, this longing for physical existence is satiated for the time, and the desire turns towards rest. Then comes the interval of disembodiment, during which the Ego, re-entering as it were into himself, ceases to energise externally on the physical plane and bends all his energies to internal activities, reviewing his gathered store of experiences, the harvest of the earth-life just closed, separating and classifying them, assimilating what is capable of assimilation, rejecting what is effete and useless. This is the work of the devachanic period, the necessary time for assimilation, for gaining equilibrium. As a workman may go out and gather the materials for his work, and having

[1] *Voice.oi the Silence*, p. 31. [2] *Ibid*

collected them may return home, sort and arrange them, and then proceed to make from them some artistic or serviceable object, so the Thinker, having gathered his store of materials from life's experiences, must weave them into the web of his millennial existence. He can no more be always busied in the whirl of earth-life than a workman can always be gathering store of materials and never fabricating from them goods; or than a man can always be eating food and never digesting it and assimilating it to build up the tissues of his body. This, with the rest needed between periods of activity by all forms of being, makes Devachan an absolute necessity, and rebukes the impatience with which ill-instructed Theosophists chafe against the idea of thus "wasting time". The rest itself is a thing, be it remembered, that we cannot do without. "The tired and worn-out Manu (thinking Ego)" needs it, and it is only "the now-rested Ego"[1] that is ready and fit for reincarnation. We have not the energy needed for taking up the burden of the flesh again until this period of refreshment has enabled the forces of life mental and spiritual to store themselves up once more in the spiritual man. It is only at the approaching close of the cycle of rebirths that the Ego, grown strong by his millenniums of experience, is able to gird himself for the awful strain of his last swiftly recurring lives, "without devachanic break," scaling those last seven steps of the ladder of existence with the tireless muscles hardened by the long ascent that lies behind.

One kind of progress—outside the necessary process of assimilation just spoken of, which is a condition of further progress—may be made in Devachan. H. P. Blavatsky says:—

[1] *Key to Theosophy*, pp. 139, 141.

In one sense, we can acquire more knowledge; that is, we can develop further any faculty which we loved and strove after during life, provided it is concerned with abstract and ideal things, such as music, painting, poetry, etc., since Devachan is merely an idealised and subjective continuation of earth-life.[1]

This may explain the marvellous infantile genius sometimes shown, especially in music, going far beyond any point known to have been reached before in the history of that art in the Aryan race. However that may be, it is well to remember that the resolute following of abstract thought, of idealistic longings, gives a trend to the devachanic state that will make it a state of active, as well as of passive, progress. While Devachan is essentially the world of effects, yet, to this extent, it borrows from the world of causes, though it is also true that the impulse must be given here which will let the wheel still turn along that peaceful road. In Devachan is no initiation of cause, no origination of endeavour, but it allows of continuation of efforts aimed at the highest planes of being that man can reach from earthly life. Why there should be this possibility it is easy to see, for the abstract and the ideal heights are illumined by the mânasic radiance, and that brightens, it is not dimmed, when Manas-Taijasi (the shining or resplendent Manas) soars unfettered to its own plane.

An interesting question arises at this juncture: when the rest-period is over, the forces that carried the Ego out of earth-life are exhausted, the longing for sentient physical existence is reviving, and the Ego ready to cross "the threshold of Devachan" and pass to the plane of reincarnation, what now guides him to the special race, nation, family, through which he is to find his new tabernacle of flesh, and what determines the sex he is to

[1] *Key to Theosophy*, p. 156.

wear? Is it affinity? Is it free choice? Is it necessity? No questions fall more readily from an inquirer's lips.

It is the law of Karma that guides him unerringly towards the race and the nation wherein are to be found the general characteristics that will produce a body, and provide a social environment, fitted for the manifestation of the general character built up by the Ego in previous earth-lives, and for the reaping of the harvest he has sown.

Karma, with its army of Skandhas, waits at the threshold of Devachan, whence the Ego re-emerges to assume a new incarnation. It is at this moment that the future destiny of the now-rested Ego trembles in the scales of just retribution, as it now falls once again under the sway of active Karmic law. It is in this rebirth which is ready for it, a rebirth selected and prepared by this mysterious, inexorable, but in the equity and wisdom of its decrees infallible LAW, that the sins of the previous life of the Ego are punished. Only it is into no imaginary Hell, with theatrical flames and ridiculous tailed and horned devils, that the Ego is cast, but verily on to this earth, the plane and region of his sins, where he will have to atone for every bad thought and deed. As he has sown, so will he reap. Reincarnation will gather around him all those other Egos who have suffered, whether directly or indirectly, at the hands, or even through the unconscious instrumentality, of the past personality. They will be thrown by Nemesis in the way of the *new* man, concealing the *old*, the eternal EGO. . . . The new "personality" is no better than a fresh suit of clothes with its specific characteristics, colour, form and qualities; but the *real* man who wears it is the same culprit as of old.[1]

Thus, say, through a militant personality in one incarnation the Ego would set up causes tending to draw him for rebirth to a race and nation passing through a militant period in its history; the Ego of a Roman of the combative colonising type would be drawn, say, to the

[1] *Key to Theosophy*, pp. 141 142

English nation under Elizabeth, a nation and epoch at which physical heredity would provide a body, and social forces an environment, fitted for the manifestation of the character built up fifteen centuries before.

Another strand in the rope of Karma, and one of the strongest, is the dominant tendency and trend of the last-closed life. Dominant tendencies and the resolute following of any line of thought and action, reappear as innate qualities. A man of strong will, who steadfastly sets himself to acquire wealth, who follows this resolve through his life relentlessly and unscrupulously, will in another incarnation be likely to be one of those men who are proverbially "lucky," of whom it is said, "everything he touches turns to gold". Hence the enormous importance of our choice of ideals, of our selection of our aim in life, for the ideals of one life become the circumstances of the next. If they are selfish, base, material, our next incarnation will bring us into an environment in which they will fall into our grasp. As an iron will compels fortune here, so it stretches its mailed grasp across the gulf of death and rebirth, and grips the end it is resolute to gain; it does not lose tension and force during the devachanic interlude, but gathers up all its energies and works in subtler matter, so that the Ego finds prepared for it on its return a tabernacle builded by that strong and passionate desire and fitted for the accomplishment of the foreseen end. *As* a man sows *so* he reaps; he is the master of his destiny, and if he wills to build for temporal success, for physical luxury, none can say him nay. Only by experience he will learn that power and wealth and luxury are but Dead-Sea fruit; that with them the body may be clothed, but the Ego will be shivering and naked; that his true self will not be satisfied with the husks that are fit food but for the swine; and at last, when he has full-fed the animal in him and starved the human, he will, though in the far country whither his wayward feet have carried him, turn yearning eyes towards his true home, and through many lives he will struggle thitherwards with all the force once used for dominance now yoked to service, and the strong man who built his strength for mastery of others will turn it to mastery of self and to training it into obedience to the Law of Love.

The question, "What determines sex?" is a difficult one to answer even by a suggestion, and definite information on this point has not been given out. The Ego itself is sexless, and each Ego, in the course of its myriad reincarnations, dwells in male and female bodies. As the building up of the perfect humanity is the object of reincarnation, and in this perfect humanity positive and negative elements must find complete equilibrium, it is easy to see that the Ego must by experience develop these characteristics to the fullest in their appropriate physical subjects, and therefore that an alternation of sexes is necessary. It is also noticeable, as a matter of observation, that at this stage of human progress advance is being made in the synthesising process, and we meet noble types of each physical sex showing some of the characteristics historically developed in the other, so that the strength, the firmness, the courage evolved along the male line are welded to the tenderness, the purity, the endurance, evolved along the female, and we catch some glimpse of what humanity shall be when the "pairs of opposites" divorced for evolution are once more united for fruition. Meanwhile it seems likely that sex-experience constantly redresses the balance of the evolutionary process, and supplies the qualities lacking at any given stage, and also that the karmic consequence of the infliction of wrong by one sex on another will be the drawing back of the wrong-doers to suffer in the wronged sex the effects of the causes they initiated.

Thus Karma traces the line which forms the Ego's path to the new incarnation, this Karma being the collectivity of causes set going by the Ego himself. In studying this play of karmic forces, however, there is one thing that ought not to be left out of account—the ready acceptance by the Ego, in his clearer-sighted vision, of conditions for his personality far other than the personality might be willing to choose for itself. The schooling of experience is not always pleasant, and to the limited knowledge of the personality there must be much of earth-experience which seems needlessly painful, unjust and useless. The Ego, ere he plunges into the "Lethe of the body," sees the causes which ultimate in the conditions of the incarnation on which he is to enter, and the opportunities which there will be therein for growth, and it is easy to realise how lightly will weigh in the balance all passing griefs and pains, how trivial, to that piercing, far-seeing gaze, the joys and woes of earth. For what is each life but a step in the

> Perpetual progress for each incarnating Ego, or divine soul, in an evolution from the outward into the inward, from the material to the Spiritual, arriving at the end of each stage at absolute unity with the Divine Principle. From strength to strength, from the beauty and perfection of one plane to the greater beauty and perfection of another, with accessions of new glory, of fresh knowledge and power in each cycle, such is the destiny of every Ego.[1]

And with such a destiny, what boots the passing suffering of a moment, or even the anguish of a darkened life?

[1] *Key to Theosophy*, p. 155.

THE PROOFS OF REINCARNATION.

The proofs of reincarnation do not amount to a complete and general demonstration, but they establish as strong a presumption as can, in the nature of the case, exist. The theory they support affords the only sufficient explanation of the growth and decay of nations, of the facts of individual evolution, of the varying capacities of man, of recurrent cycles in history, of unique human characters. I am content—despite my own certain knowledge that reincarnation is a fact in nature—to present it here as a reasonable working hypothesis, rather than as a demonstrated theorem; for I am writing for those who are seeking evidence in the facts of human life and history, and for them it cannot at first rise beyond the position of a reasonable hypothesis. Those who know it to be true need no arguments from me.

i. There are some living persons, as well as some not at present in earth-life, who remember their own past incarnations, and can recall their incidents as they can recall those of their present lives. Memory—which is the link between the varying stages of experience of the conscious being, and which carries with it the sense of individuality and of personality alike—stretches for them through the gateways of past births and deaths, and the nights of death no more break the chain of memory than the nights break it which separate the days of our ordinary life. Occurrences of their past lives are as real experiences of their living selves as though they had happened a few years agone, and to tell them that they did not have these experiences is a view to them as foolish as if you persisted that the events they passed through ten years ago happened to somebody else and not to their same selves. They would not debate the question with you, but would just shrug their shoulders and drop the subject, for you cannot argue a man's own experience out of his consciousness. On the other hand, a man's testimony to facts within his own knowledge cannot demonstrate the reality of those facts to a second person, and therefore this evidence is not conclusive proof to any one but the experiencer. It is the final certainty of the truth of reincarnation to the person whose memory bears this witness to his own past; its value to the hearer must depend on that hearer's opinion of the intellectual sanity and moral worth of the speaker. If the speaker be a person of not only ordinary sanity in the affairs of everyday life, but of supreme intellectual strength; a person of not only ordinary morality, but of lofty moral purity, veracity and accuracy; under such circumstances his deliberate statement that he remembers incidents of his own life happening, say, some centuries ago, and his relation of these incidents with their local surroundings in detail, would probably have considerable weight with those familiar with his integrity and ability; it is second-hand evidence, but good of its kind.

ii. The vegetable, the animal, the man, all show signs of the working of the "law of heredity," of the tendency of parents to transmit to their offspring peculiarities of their own organisation. The oak, the dog, the man, are recognisable, under superficial divergences, all the world over. All are generated and grow along definite lines; from two cells, a male and a female, each proceeds, developing along the lines of the parental characteristics. The offspring reproduce the specific parental marks, and however widely families of the same type may differ, we yet recognise the uniting peculiarities. We unite under the name of "dog" the St. Bernard and the toy-terrier, the boarhound and the Italian greyhound, as we unite under the name of "man" the Veddah and the Englishman, the Negro and the Râjput. But when we come to deal with intellectual and moral capacities, say in varieties of dogs and of men, we are struck with a significant difference. In the dog these vary between comparatively narrow limits; he may be clever or stupid, vicious or reliable, but the difference between a clever and a stupid dog is comparatively small. But in man how huge is the distance which separates the lowest from the highest, whether intellectually or morally: one race can only count "one, two, three, many," while the sons of another can calculate distances that have to be reckoned in light-years; one race counts it as filial virtue to slay its parents, or regards treachery as righteous, while another gives to humanity a Francis Xavier, a Howard, a Lloyd Garrison. In man, and in man only, among all the races that people earth, do we find such great physical unity and such vast intellectual and moral divergence. I admit physical heredity as explanation of the one, but I need some new factor, not present in the brute, as an explanation of the other. Reincarnation, with its persistent intellectual and moral Ego, learning by experience, developing through millenniums, offers a sufficient cause; and a cause which also explains why man progresses while animals remain stationary, from the mental and moral standpoint, save as artificially bred and trained by man. As far back as records reach, wild animals have lived as they live now, beasts of prey, herds of buffaloes, tribes of monkeys, communities of ants; they live and die, generation after generation, repeating parental habits, slipping along ancestral grooves, evolving no higher social life. They have physical heredity as man has, but physical heredity does not—for it cannot—give them the accumulated experience which enables the persistent human Egos to climb onwards ever, building great civilisations, gathering knowledge, rising higher and higher, so that none can trace a limit beyond which Humanity cannot grow. It is this persistent element, lacking in the animal and present in the man, that explains why the animal is comparatively stationary and the man progressive. There is no individual store-house for the experience gathered by the animal; but man, storing the essence of his experience in the immortal Ego, starts life after life with this store as his possession, and so has the possibility of continued individual growth. For how can intellectual experience be transmitted, save by consciousness? Physical habits, which modify the organism, can be physically transmitted, as the tendency to trot in the horse, to point in the dog, and so on; in animals and in men alike, these facts are notorious. Equally notorious is the fact of the intellectual and moral stagnation of the animal as compared with the progressiveness of man. Another noteworthy fact is that no outside influence can impress on the brains of the lowest human races the elementary moral conceptions, which the brains of the more advanced assimilate almost immediately on presentation. Something more than the brain-apparatus is necessary for an intellectual or moral perception, and no training can give this something; training may render delicate the apparatus, but the impulse from the Ego is needed ere that apparatus can answer to the prompting from without. Nor does it tell against this truth that a European child, shut out of all human companionship, was found to be brutish and scarcely human on his release; for the physical organ needs the healthy play upon it of physical influences, if it is to be used on the physical plane, and if it is disorganised by unnatural treatment it cannot answer to any promptings from the Ego, any more than a piano, left to damp and rust, can give out melodious notes from its injured strings.

iii. Within the limits of a family there are certain hereditary peculiarities which continually reappear, and a certain "family likeness" unites the members of a family. These physical resemblances are patent, and are looked upon as evidences of the law of heredity. So far, good. But what law explains the startling divergences in mental capacity and moral character that are found within the narrow limits of a single family circle, among the children of the same parents? In a family of quiet, home-loving people, settled on the same spot for generations, is born a lad of wild and roving spirit, that no discipline can tame, no lure can hold. How can such a type be found in such surroundings, if the mental and the moral nature be born of ancestral sources? Or a "black sheep" is born in a pure and noble family, wringing the hearts that love him, dishonouring a spotless name; whence comes he? Or a white blossom of saintliness unfolds its radiant beauty amid sordid and gross family surroundings; what dropped seed of that exquisite plant into soil so evil? Here, in every case, reincarnation gives the clue, placing the mental and moral qualities in the immortal Ego, not in the physical body born of the parents. Strong physical likeness is found between brothers whose mental and moral characters are as the poles asunder. Heredity may explain the one; it cannot explain the other.[1] Reincarnation steps in to fill the gap, and so renders complete the theory of human growth.

[1] I am not forgetting "reversion," nor the question of how these discordant types enter a family if the Egos are drawn, as said, to suitable surroundings, but these points will be dealt with under "objections".

iv. This same problem is presented even more strongly in the case of twins, in which the children have not only identical ancestry, but identical pre-natal conditions. Yet twins often unite the most complete physical likeness with strong difference of mental and moral type. And another matter of significance in connection with twins is that during infancy they will often be indistinguishable from each other, even to the keen eye of mother and of nurse. Whereas, later in life, when Manas has been working through his physical encasement, he will have so modified it that the physical likeness lessens and the differences of character stamp themselves on the mobile features.

v. Infant precocity demands some explanation at the hands of science. Why can a Mozart, at four, show knowledge in which none has trained him? Not only taste for melody, but "instinctive" ability to produce settings for melodies given him, settings which break none of the complicated laws of harmony that the musician has to learn by patient study. "He was born of a musical family." Surely; otherwise it is hard to see how the delicate physical apparatus necessary for the manifestation of his transcendent genius could have been provided; but if his family gave him the genius as well as the physical machinery for its manifestation, one would like to know why so many shared in the possession of the physical musical apparatus, while none save he showed the power that welled up in the symphonies, the sonatas, the operas, the masses, that flowed in jewelled cascades from that exhaustless source. How could effect so mighty flow from cause so inadequate? for among all the Mozart family there was only one MOZART. And many another case might be quoted in which the child outran its teachers, doing with ease what they had accomplished with toil, and quickly doing what they could in no wise accomplish.

vi. Infant precocity is but a form of manifestation of genius, and genius itself needs explanation. Whence comes it, harder to trace than the track of birds in the air? A Plato, a Dante, a Bruno, a Shakespeare, a Newton; whence are they, these radiant children of Humanity? They spring from mediocre families, the first and the last to make the name immortal, families whose very obscurity is the definite proof that they possess but average abilities; a child is born, loved, caressed, punished, educated, like all the others; suddenly the young eagle soars aloft to the sun from the house-sparrow's nest beneath the eaves, and the beat of his wings shakes the very air. Did such a thing happen on the physical plane we should not murmur, "Heredity and a curious case of reversion"; we should seek the parent eagle, not trace the genealogy of the sparrows. And so, when the strong Ego stoops to the mediocre family, we must seek in that Ego the cause of the genius, not look for it in the family genealogy.

Will any one venture to explain by heredity the birth into the world of a great moral genius, a Lao-Tze, a Buddha, a Zarathushtra, a Jesus? Is the divine root whence spring these blossoms of humanity to be dug for in the soil of physical ancestry, the sources of their gracious lives in the small well of commonplace humanity? Whence brought they their untaught wisdom, their spiritual insight, their knowledge of human sorrows and human needs? Men have been so dazzled by their teaching that they have dreamed it a revelation from a supernatural Deity, while it is the ripened fruit of hundreds of human lives; those who reject the supernatural Deity must either accept reincarnation or accept the insolubility of the problem of their origin. If heredity can produce Buddhas and Christs, it might well give us more of them.

vii. We are led to the same conclusion by noting the extraordinary differences between people in the power of assimilating knowledges of various kinds. Take two persons of some intellectual power, clever rather than stupid. Present to each the same system of philosophy. One swiftly grasps its main principles, the other remains passive and inert before it. Present to the same two some other system, and their relative positions will be reversed. One "has a bent" towards one form of thought, the second towards some other. Two students are attracted to Theosophy and begin to study it; at a year's end one is familiar with its main conceptions and can apply them, while the other is struggling in a maze. To the one each principle seemed familiar on presentation; to the other, new, unintelligible, strange. The believer in reincarnation understands that the teaching is old to the one and new to the other; one learns quickly *because he remembers*, he is but recovering past knowledge; the other learns slowly because his experience has not included these truths of nature, and he is acquiring them toilfully for the first time.

viii. Closely allied to this rapid recovery of past knowledge is the intuition which perceives a truth as true on its presentation, and needs no slow process of argument for arrival at conviction. Such intuition is merely recognition of a fact familiar in a past life, though met for the first time in the present. Its mark is that no argument strengthens the internal conviction which came with the mere perception of the fact; arguments demonstrating its reality may be sought and built up for the sake of others, but they are not needed for the satisfaction of the believer himself. *That* work has been done, so far as he is concerned, in his own previous experience, and he has no need to retravel the same road.

ix. Reincarnation solves, as does no other theory of human existence, the problems of inequality of circumstances, of capacity, of opportunity, which otherwise remain as evidence that justice is not a factor in life, but that men are the mere sport of the favouritism of an irresponsible Creator, or of the blind forces of a soulless Nature. A child is born with a brain fitted to be the instrument of all animal passions, a "criminal brain," the vehicle of evil desires, brutal instinct; child of a thief and a harlot, his life-blood flows from a foul and poisoned source; his surroundings educate him to vicious courses, train him in all evil ways. Another is born with a nobly moulded brain, fitted to manifest the most splendid intellect, with small physical substratum as basis and instrument for brutal passions; child of pure and thoughtful parents, his physical nature is built of good materials, and his surroundings push him along right paths of conduct, training him to good and generous action, helping him to repress all base and evil thoughts. The one by organism and environment is foredoomed to a life of crime, or, at best, if the Divine in him should make itself felt, to a terrific struggle against enormous odds, a struggle which, even should it end in victory, must leave the victor exhausted, maimed, heartbroken. The other by organism and environment is foredoomed to a life of beneficent activity, and his struggle will be not against the evil that drags him down but after the higher good that allures him upwards. Whence such diverse fates, if these human beings enter for the first time on life's stage? Shall we say that some conscious and overruling Providence creates two lives, banning the one to uttermost degradation, blessing the other to loftiest possibilities? If so, then a wailing and helpless Humanity, in the grip of a fathomless Injustice, can but shudder and submit, but must cease to speak of Justice or of Love as being attributes of the Deity it worships. If a similar result come about by the blind forces of Nature, then also is man helpless in the grasp of causes he can neither fathom nor control, and round his heart, while his race endures, must coil the fanged serpent of poisonous resentment against injustice, good and evil lots being ground out of the lottery-wheel of blinded Fortune, lots which fall into men's laps without power of theirs to accept or to reject. But if reincarnation be true, Justice rules the world and man's destiny lies in his own hands. The yielding to evil thoughts and acts, the infliction of wrong on others, the unscrupulous pursuance of selfish ends, these build up for the reincarnating Man a brain which is the fitted instrument for their increased manifestation, a brain in which all evil tendencies will find grooves ready for their easy working, and in which good forces will seek in vain physical organs for their expression. The nature with such evil physical equipment will be drawn to suitable environment, where opportunities for evil action offer themselves on every hand, to parents whose poisoned bodies can yield the physical materials most fitted to serve as substratum for such manifestation. Terrible? Aye, just as it is terrible that persistent drunkenness should lead to destruction of body and brain. But where there is justice, inviolable Law, there is hope, for we are then no mere straws, driven by the wind, but masters of our own fate, since by knowledge we can use these laws, which never fail us, and which become our helpers instead of our foes. For as man may build to evil, he may build to good, and the reverse of the results just sketched may be brought about. Resistance of wrong thought and act, patient service of others, scrupulous devotion to unselfish ends, these build up for the reincarnating Man a brain which is the fitted instrument for their increased manifestation, in which all good tendencies will find grooves ready for their easy working, and in which evil forces will seek in vain physical organs for their expression. Such a nature is equally drawn to environment where opportunities for good will crowd around it, to parents worthy to build its physical tabernacle. But in each case the tabernacle is built on the plan supplied by the architect, the Ego, and he is responsible for his work.[1]

Again, reincarnation explains to us the extraordinary contrasts between people's aspirations and their capacities. We find an eager mind imprisoned in a most inefficient body, and we know it is hampered now by its sloth in utilising capacities in a previous life. We find another yearning after the very loftiest attainments, struggling with pathetic eagerness to grasp the subtlest conceptions, while it lamentably fails to assimilate the most elementary and fundamental ideas of the philosophy it would master, or to fulfil the humble requirements of a fairly unselfish and useful life. We recognise that in the past opportunities have been wasted, possibilities of great attainments disregarded or wilfully rejected, so that now the Ego's upward path is hindered and his strength is crippled, and the soul yearns with pitiful and hopeless eagerness for knowledge, not denied it by any outside power, but unattainable because it cannot see it, though it lies at its very feet.

[1]It must never be forgotten that worldly rank, wealth, etc., do not run on all fours with good and evil surroundings. In the first extreme case sketched in the text, the surroundings are distinctly evil, but in the second case the Ego might be surrounded by worldly troubles just because it had won the right to have opportunities of growth.

There is another suggestion that may appeal to those who believe in a personal overruling Providence, who creates the spirits of men. Is it seemly to imagine Deity as at the beck and call of His creatures in the exercise of His creative energy, as waiting attendant on the passions and lusts of men to create a human spirit to inhabit the body which springs from some evil act of unbridled self-indulgence? This constant creation of new spirits to inhabit forms dependent for their existence on man's caprice has in it something which must be repugnant to those who reverence their ideal of a Divine Being. Yet there is no other alternative, if they believe man is a spirit—or has a spirit, as they mostly phrase it—and reject reincarnation.[1]

x. Another argument which appeals only to those who believe in the immortality of man is that all which begins in time ends in time. All that has a beginning has an ending, and the necessary correlative of immortality after death is eternal existence before birth. This is why Hume declared that metempsychosis was the only theory of the soul to which philosophy could hearken, since "what is incorruptible must be ungenerable". Thought which rises to the dignity of philosophy must accept either reincarnation, or the cessation of individual existence at death.

xi. Yet, again, is it not somewhat irrational, given the immortality of the spiritual Intelligence in man, to suppose that such an Intelligence comes into the world, inhabits, say, the body of a Fiji Islander, leaves it, and never returns to learn the innumerable lessons this earthly life can teach, but has not yet taught him? We see how much more of growth, mental and moral, is

[1] See Prof. W. Knight's Essay in the *Fortnightly Review*, Sept., 1878.

possible for man on earth than that accomplished by a Fiji Islander. Why should that Intelligence finally quit earth-life until all its lessons have been mastered? To send on that inexperienced Intelligence into some higher sphere of spiritual life is like sending on a boy in the lowest class of a school to the university. Common-sense bids him return for term after term, after the rest of the holidays, until he reaches the highest class, and passes from that, having learned what the school has to teach him, to the wider life and deeper learning of the college.

xii. Analogy suggests the co-existence of the temporary and permanent elements in one life-cycle. The leaves of a tree are born, mature, and fall; during their life they take in nourishment, change it into substances useful to the tree, transmit the result of their life-energy to the tree, and—die. They do not rise again, but the tree endures, and puts out with the new spring a new crop of leaves. So does the personality live, gather in experience, transmute it into permanent values, transmit it to the enduring tree whence it springs, and then perish; after the winter passes, the Ego puts forth the new personality to do similar work, and so to build up and nourish the growth of the tree of Man. And so all through nature we see the temporary serving the permanent, working for the growth of that more enduring life of which it is itself but the passing expression.

xiii. The recurring cycles of history point to the re-incarnation of large numbers of persons as it were in bulk. We find at the close of periods of fifteen centuries the re-emergence of the types of intelligence and of character that marked the beginnings of such periods. Let the student, with this idea in his mind, compare the Augustan period of Roman history with the Elizabethan period of English. Let him compare the conquering, colonising, empire-building type of the Romans with that of the English. Let him compare the currents of religious thought in the third and fourth centuries after Christ with those of the eighteenth and nineteenth, and see if he cannot trace in the prevalence of mystic and Gnostic thought to-day any re-emergence from the close of the fourth century. When he has pursued this line of study for a while, he will begin to see that the statement in Theosophical books that fifteen centuries is the "average period between incarnations" is not a mere fancy or guess.

xiv. The rise and decay of races is best explained on the hypothesis of reincarnation. It is noticed that some races are dying out, despite the efforts which have been made to check their decay; their women become afflicted with sterility and so their numbers steadily diminish, their complete extinction being only a question of time. The reincarnationist says: "The Egos are leaving that race; all that can be learned through that particular expression has been learned; the Egos that once informed its children have gone on into other races; there are no more baby Egos to puzzle out through it the lessons of their earliest human experience; hence there is no demand on it from the plane of causes, and it must inevitably disappear". So also do we find that when a race has reached its acme of attainment slow decline sets in, and synchronously another race begins its upgrowth and rises as the other falls. For the advanced Egos, having used a racial type to its utmost possibilities, seek then another type with higher possibilities before it, and leaving the less advanced Egos to incarnate in the first type they themselves pass on to a younger race; and so the succession goes on, less and less advanced

Egos incarnating in the first type, which therefore slowly degenerates, until the stage spoken of above is reached and signs of approaching extinction are seen.

Many another proof of the reality of reincarnation might be brought forward, but with our limited space these must suffice. The earnest and painstaking student can add others, as his knowledge grows.

Objections to Reincarnation.

The statement of objections here adduced is drawn from those raised by opponents and inquirers, and is merely offered as a sample of those most frequently met.

i. *The Loss of Memory.* This is fully dealt with under the heading What it is that does not reincarnate, and the explanation need not be repeated here.

ii. *The Increase of Population.* If the number of Egos, it is asked, be a fixed number, how do you account for the increase of population? It is a doubtful matter, to begin with, whether there is, or is not, an increase of the total population of the globe, however great may be the increase on any particular area. No census of the total population has ever been taken, no statistics are available for our guidance. But let us take it for granted that there is an increase of the total population. This is perfectly consistent with a growth in the number of the incarnated Egos, seeing the small proportion these bear to the total number of Egos out of incarnation. To reduce the answer to a very concrete form: there are three thousand Egos to be incarnated; one hundred are incarnated, leaving two thousand nine hundred out of incarnation; a period of fifteen hundred years is to elapse before the first hundred come into incarnation again, and so with each successive hundred; a very slight shortening of the period out of incarnation for some must vastly increase the incarnated population. Those who raise this objection generally take it for granted that the proportion of Egos out of incarnation to those in incarnation is about half and half, whereas the number out of incarnation is enormously greater than that of the Egos incarnated. The globe is as a small hall in a large town, drawing the audiences that enter it from the total population. It may be at one time half empty, at another crowded, without any change in the total population of the town. So our little globe may be thinly or thickly populated, and the vast number of Egos on which it draws to replenish its stock of inhabitants remains practically inexhaustible.

iii. *Reincarnation ignores the Law of Heredity.* On the contrary, it enforces it on the physical plane. It admits that the parents in giving the physical materials stamp these with their own signet, so to speak, and that the molecules built into the child's body carry with them the habit of vibrating in definite ways and of associating themselves in particular combinations. Thus will be conveyed hereditary diseases; thus will be transmitted little tricks of manner, habits, gestures, etc. "But," the objector proceeds, "this is not all. Mental likenesses are transmitted, mental peculiarities as well as physical." This is true within limits, but not to the extent taken for granted by those who would fain explain everything by the working of a single law. Etheric atoms as well as physical are contributed by the parents, as are also kâmic elements—especially by the mother—and these work on the molecules of the brain as well as on those of the rest of the body, and so cause the reappearance in the child of vital and passional characteristics of the parents, modifying the manifestations of the Thinker, the Manas, the reincarnating Ego. The theory of reincarnation admits all these modes of influence by the parents on the child, but while allowing to the fullest for these, it refuses to ignore all the independent action of which exist proofs as striking as those of parental influence on the Lower Quaternary, and so Theosophy gives a full explanation of differences and of similarities, whereas heredity gives only a partial and one-sided one, laying stress on the similarities and ignoring the differences.

iv. *Reversion is sufficient to explain the differences*, is the answer to the last criticism; genius is explained by reversion, as are all types wholly different from the immediate progenitors. But if genius be a case of reversion then we ought to be able to recognise the ancestor endowed with it, since it marks out its possessor from the crowd. Genius should only appear, however long the intervals, in families in which it has already been manifested. If Shakespeare be an instance of reversion, to whom did he revert? The very fact that a genius suddenly renders illustrious a family hitherto obscure negates the hypothesis of reversion, since the obscurity is itself the guarantee of the absence of genius. It may also be remarked that when the birth of a vicious child in a virtuous family is put down to reversion, the explanation is a pure guess without a shadow of proof in its support. If genius could be established as a reversion, then, by analogy, the other cases might be similarly argued for, but where the presumption is against this explanation in the case in which it might easily be verified, if true, little stress can be laid on it in cases in which verification is almost necessarily impossible.

v. *The appearance of a vicious child in a virtuous family, and of a virtuous child in a vicious family, is against the theory that the Ego is drawn to those who can give it a suitable body and environment.* At the first blush, this objection seems a strong one, but it leaves out of account the very important question of karmic ties. The Esoteric Philosophy teaches that the future destinies of Egos become intertwined by the relations set up between them in any earth-life. Love and hatred, service and injury, comradeship in good and evil, all tend to draw the Egos back to earth-life together, for the joint working out of effects jointly caused. Hence the shocking, and on this plane unnatural, hatreds found to exist sometimes between parents and children, brothers and sisters—hatreds as inexplicable as they are malignant, marked with monstrous features of revenge as for some unremembered but dominating wrong. Hence, too, the inseverable ties that bind hearts together, out-reaching distance, out-lasting time, ties whose uncaused strength in this life points to a genesis beyond the portal of birth.

A Last Word.

And here must end this imperfect treatment of a theme too vast and too deep for pen feeble as mine. This sketch can but serve as elementary introduction to a study of one of the weightiest problems of human existence, a study more vital, perchance, to our present stage of civilisation than any other in which the mind of man can engage. All life changes its aspect when reincarnation becomes a deeply settled conviction, beyond all argument, raised above all dispute. Each day of life but one page in the great drama of existence; each sorrow but the fleeting shadow cast by a passing cloud; each joy but a gleam of sunshine reflected from a swinging mirror;

each death but the moving from a worn-out house. The strength of an eternal youth begins slowly to pass into the awakening life; the calmness of a vast serenity broods over the tossing waves of human thought; the radiant glory of the immortal Intelligence pierces the thick dusky clouds of matter, and the imperishable Peace that nought can ruffle sheds its pure whiteness over the triumphant spirit. Pinnacle after pinnacle of spiritual heights lift themselves into the illimitable ether, steps which climb the azure immeasurable, and fade into the infinite distance which shrouds the Future, immense and unimaginable by the very spirit in man. And then, "blinded by the excess of light," wrapped in a hope too deep to be joyous, too sure to be triumphant, too vast to be syllabled, Man enters into the All-consciousness to which our consciousness is as senselessness, till Eternity again thrills with the summons, COME FORTH, FOR THE DAY OF BRAHMÂ IS DAWNING AND THE NEW WHEEL BEGINS TO TURN!

PEACE TO ALL BEINGS.